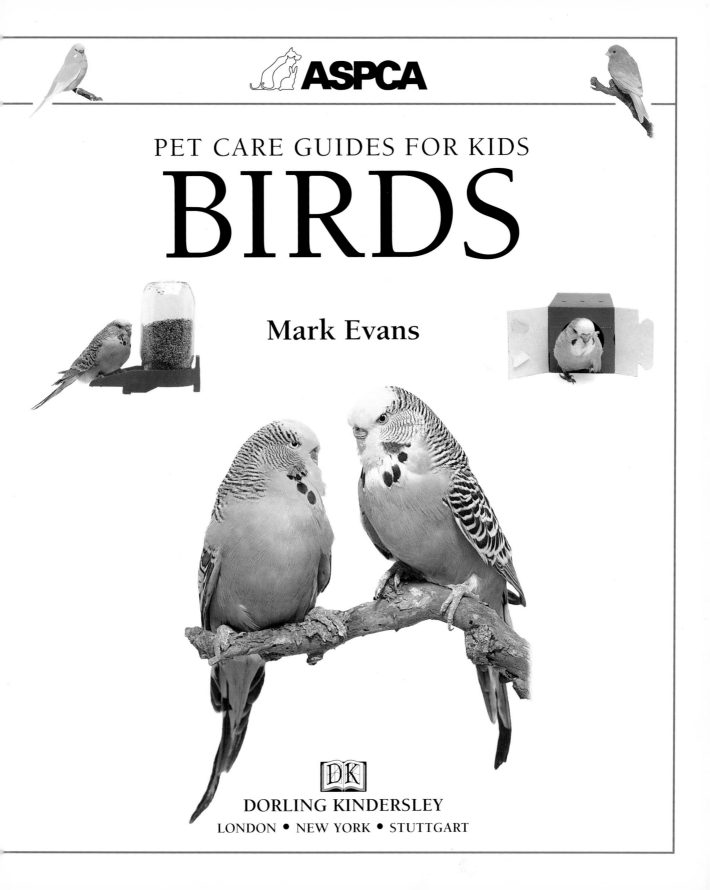

PET CARE GUIDES FOR KIDS

BIRDS

Mark Evans

ASPCA

DORLING KINDERSLEY

LONDON • NEW YORK • STUTTGART

A DORLING KINDERSLEY BOOK

Project Editor Liza Bruml
Art Editor Sarah Ponder
Editor Miriam Farbey
U.S. Editor B. Alison Weir
Photographer Paul Bricknell
Additional photography Frank Greenaway
and Cyril Laubscher
Illustrator Peter Visscher
ASPCA Consultant Stephen Zawistowski, Ph.D.

First American Edition, 1993
2 4 6 8 10 9 7 5 3 1

Published in the United States by
Dorling Kindersley, Inc., 232 Madison Avenue
New York, New York 10016

Library of Congress Cataloging-in-Publication Data
Evans, Mark, 1962-
    Birds / by Mark Evans : foreword by Roger Caras. — 1st American
ed.
        p.   cm. — (ASPCA pet care guides for kids)
    Includes index.
    Summary: A guide to caring for bird pets.
    ISBN 1-56458-271-X
    1. Cage birds—Juvenile literature.   [1. Birds as pets.]
I. Title.   II. Series.
SF461.35.E93 1993
636.6'8—dc20   92-54621
                                                            CIP
                                                            AC

Models: Jacob Brubert, Adam Conduct, Arron Daubney, Luke Harris, Naoka
Hoshika, Sarah-Louise Hurtley, Fiona Lala, Nicola Mason, Carlie and Lee
Nicolls, Danny O'Sullivan, Kim and Lee Robertson

Dorling Kindersley would like to thank Ernie Sigston for
providing budgies and equipment, Concepta Keenan for lending her budgie,
The Junior Bird League, Pedigree Pet Foods for supplying bird seed, Tracy
White for design help, Salvo Tomasselli for the world map and
Lynn Bresler for the index.

Picture credits: OSF/RJB Goodale Ace Films Australia p12 tr

Color reproduction by Colourscan, Singapore
Printed and bound in Italy by Arnoldo Mondadori, Verona

Foreword

Birds are among the most beautiful
creatures on Earth. There are about
9,000 different kinds and each species
has special needs. Any bird you keep as
a pet will suffer from dampness and
cold, especially from drafts. The wrong
site for even a short time can kill a cage
bird. Neither do birds like sudden,
loud noises or too much
excitement. Plenty
of the right kinds
of food, fresh water,
and a clean place to
perch and sleep can
keep a bird happy for
many years—and
what wonderful pets
they are!

Roger Caras *ASPCA President*

Note to parents
This book teaches your child how to be
a caring and responsible pet owner. But
remember, your child must have your
help and guidance in every aspect of day-
to-day pet care. Don't let your child keep
birds unless you are sure that your family
has the time and resources to look after
them properly—for the whole of
their lives.

Contents

Introduction

The first step to becoming a good bird owner is to choose the right number and kind of pets. Budgies are the easiest to look after. A budgie likes to have company, so you should get at least two. But remember: whatever kinds and however many pets you choose, you'll need to care for them every day. Not just to start with, but for the whole of their lives.

Understanding your pets

You have to get to know your birds. If you handle them gently and talk to them as much as you can, they will quickly learn to trust you. Watch them very carefully and you will soon begin to understand the many fascinating things that they do.

Shopping basket full of things you will need

Budgies sleep with their heads tucked into their wings

Your birds enjoy a weekly shower

Caring for your pets

You will only be your pets' best friend if you care for them properly. They need water, the right food, and lots of flying exercise every day. You will have to clean the cage regularly and spray your birds once a week.

Taking your hobby further

Once you have learned how to care for budgies, you may want to keep other kinds of pet birds. If you have a space outside, you could set up an aviary.

Fawn penguin zebra finches make good pets

People to help

The best bird-keeper always tries to find out more about her pets. The veterinarian at your local animal clinic will check that your birds are healthy. Ask him anything you like about how to keep your birds healthy.

You should visit your veterinarian often

New family members

Your birds will be a special part of your family. Everyone will want to join in training and looking after them. Your birds may become friends with other small pets. You can also introduce them to friends that like animals.

Your birds will be part of your family

Ask a grown-up

👥When you see this sign in the book, you should ask an adult to help you.

Things to remember

When you live with pet birds, there are some important rules you should follow:

🐦 Never allow your pet birds to fly free outside.

🐦 Wash your hands after handling your birds or cleaning their cage.

🐦 Don't kiss your birds.

🐦 Always handle your birds very gently.

🐦 Never tease or poke your birds; it's cruel.

🐦 Don't give your birds food from your plate.

What is a bird?

Birds belong to a large group of animals that have a backbone, called vertebrates. All birds are warm-blooded and their young hatch from eggs. Their light bodies are covered with feathers. Instead of arms they have wings that they usually use for flying. They take off, steer, and land with more control than any airplane. The most popular pet bird, the budgerigar (also called a budgie or parakeet), belongs to a group of birds called parrots. All parrots have short, hooked beaks for cracking open seeds.

Wing is powered by strong chest muscles

Wing flaps to keep the bird up and moving

Head feathers are deep and soft

Eye on side of head looks out for danger

Small nostril

Waxy cere

Strong beak does not contain any teeth

Horny beak grows constantly

Neck feathers are called the mask

Built to fly

A budgie is perfectly made for flying. Its streamlined body has hollow bones and its skull contains air spaces to make it light. A budgie has a special way of breathing that allows it to get a lot of oxygen to its main flight muscles. These large muscles power the wings to lift the bird into the air. The feathers that make up a bird's plumage are called tail, body, wing, and down feathers.

Super senses

A bird has keen eyesight to make sure that it doesn't bump into things when flying fast. It has very good hearing, although you can't see its ear flaps. The cere, the waxy swelling at the top of its beak, has two small holes that are the bird's nostrils. But budgies have a poor sense of smell and taste.

Long, pointed tail feathers are used for steering and keeping the bird stable

Short secondary flight feathers give the wing a smooth, curved surface

Long primary feathers steer and power flight

The amazing variety of birds

Fluffy down feathers help keep the bird warm

Stubby alula helps keep the wing stable

Black stripes are called bars

Pointed head is a stream-lined shape

The huge ostrich cannot fly.

A penguin swims with paddle-shaped wings.

Eye has white iris ring

Black markings are called neck spots

A duck uses its webbed back feet like flippers.

Smooth body feathers are waterproof

Legs are held close to the body

Wings are held neatly against the body

Powerful wings let the swift stay in the air for a long time.

Claws dig into perch

Legs are covered in scaly skin

Perching

Small tail feathers fan out to act as a brake

A budgie lands on a branch to rest, or perch. Each leg has four claws. Two claws face forward and two face backward to give the bird a strong grip. A bird can even perch upside down!

Long tail is used for balance

The gorgeous colors in the male peacock's tail attract a mate.

11

Life in the wild

Wild budgerigars live in the dry grasslands of Australia. They are nomadic, which means that they never settle in one place. Nearly all wild budgies are yellow and green colored so they are hidden when they feed in grass. They live in large groups, called flocks. Although the budgie is the most popular pet bird, it is not the only one. Over thousands of years many kinds of wild birds, from all over the world, have been tamed.

Finding food and drink
Budgies eat wild grass seeds and drink from desert pools in the cool early morning and evening. The flocks fly from place to place in search of food and water.

Life in the flock
A flock of budgies may have only 20 birds, but if food or water is scarce, thousands of birds will join together. A large group is better at protecting itself from enemies and finding food and water. The flock sleeps, or roosts, in the safety of the high branches.

Small, wild budgie is yellow and green

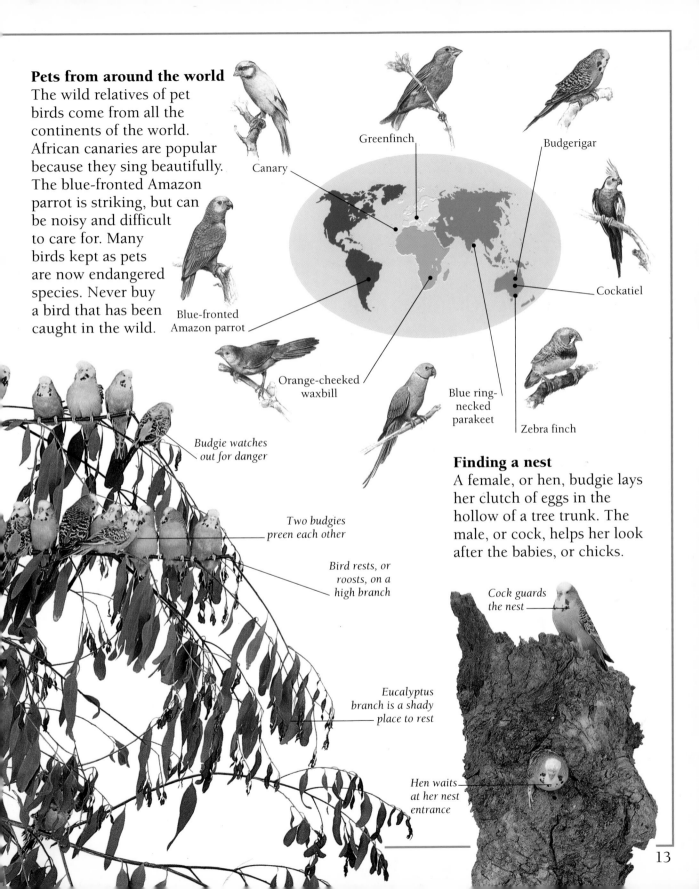

Pets from around the world

The wild relatives of pet birds come from all the continents of the world. African canaries are popular because they sing beautifully. The blue-fronted Amazon parrot is striking, but can be noisy and difficult to care for. Many birds kept as pets are now endangered species. Never buy a bird that has been caught in the wild.

Canary

Greenfinch

Budgerigar

Cockatiel

Blue-fronted Amazon parrot

Orange-cheeked waxbill

Blue ring-necked parakeet

Zebra finch

Budgie watches out for danger

Two budgies preen each other

Bird rests, or roosts, on a high branch

Finding a nest

A female, or hen, budgie lays her clutch of eggs in the hollow of a tree trunk. The male, or cock, helps her look after the babies, or chicks.

Cock guards the nest

Eucalyptus branch is a shady place to rest

Hen waits at her nest entrance

13

Types of budgies

The first people to keep budgies noticed that some chicks had unusual markings and feather colors. By choosing which of these to breed, the bird-keepers created different types of budgies. Today, there are hundreds of types. They can be divided into groups according to their color and markings.

Yellow forehead

Yellow and green wings with black markings

Light green

The wild budgie
Most wild budgies are green with black wing markings and yellow faces. All green budgies have yellow faces.

Other normals
Budgies with black wing markings are called normals. Their bodies can be different colors, such as gray or blue. They can have either white or yellow faces.

Cinnamon violet

Brown lines on wings

Cinnamon sky blue

Throat spots are brown

Light gray chest

White head

Normal sky blue

Normal gray

Deep blue chest

Pink feet

Bright yellow face

Violet body

Normal cobalt

Cinnamon gray-green

Cinnamon light green

Normal yellow-faced violet

Cinnamon gray

Tail is cinnamon

Cinnamons
Some budgies have brown markings on their wings and throat spots. They are called cinnamons. Their bodies can be any color but they are not as bright as normals.

Graywings
Graywing budgies are rare. They have gray instead of black wing markings. Their bodies are different colors, but are always very pale.

Fine gray lines on wing

Pale sky blue body

Graywinged sky blue

Gray feet

Long light blue tail

White band

Faint black markings

Cere has pink tinge

Black-tipped wing feathers

Sky blue dominant pied

White patch

Opaline violet

Cinnamon gray dominant pied

Violet recessive pied

Light green spangle

Red eye

Pink cere

White body

Pink feet

White cheek patch

Albino

Body patterns
The dominant pied budgie has patches or a band of a different color. The cere and feet of a recessive pied are tinted with pink and it has no iris ring. A budgie with faint black markings on its neck, back, and the rear of its head is called an opaline. The spangle has dark-edged, pale wing feathers.

Lutino

White tail

Yellow face

A single color
All the feathers of the albino are white. Its eyes, cere, and feet are pink. The lutino is completely yellow apart from its tail, cheeks, and wing tips.

Brown spots

White-edged throat spots

Dark-edged wing feather

Amazing mixtures
Some birds look unusual because they have a mixture of many features. They are impossible to put into one class.

Yellow-faced albino

Yellow-faced opaline cinnamon sky blue

Opaline spangle cobalt

15

Your budgies' home

Your budgies need a large cage to live in so they have plenty of room to stretch their wings. Put the cage in a safe place in your living room, where your budgies will often have company. You will also need to buy feeding equipment, lining material for the cage trays, and a cage cover. Stock up with food and find branches to use as perches.

Bars are 3/8 in (10 mm) apart to prevent your birds from poking their heads through

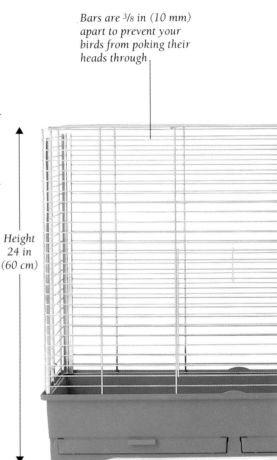

Height 24 in (60 cm)

Length: 26 in (65 cm)

The cage
Look at the measurements in the picture. Your pets' cage should be at least this big, and wider than it is tall so that your birds can fly between the perches. The cage bars must be horizontal so your birds can exercise by climbing them.

Lining paper

Bird sand-sheet

Wood shavings

Storage bin

Scoop

Bird sand

Fruit-tree perch
Find branches for perches that are at least 3/8 in (10 mm) wide.

Lining the cage
Buy paper and wood shavings to line the trays. To give your birds something different to stand on sometimes, get bird sand-sheets or sand.

Cage cover
Make or buy a cover to put over the cage so your birds can rest.

16

Check the measurements of a cage before buying it

Tray slides open so cage lining can be easily replaced

Water drinker

Feeding perch

Jam-jar seed hopper

Fresh food tray   Grit hopper

Feeding equipment

You will need containers for water, seed, grit, and fresh food. Buy hoppers with perches for your birds to stand on while they eat.

Clips

Buy some clips to attach food and the cuttlefish to the cage bars.

Food and minerals

Buy an all-in-one budgerigar seed mixture, soluble grit, cuttlefish, and a small iodine block. Store the seed and grit in air-tight containers. You will also need to feed your birds fresh foods (see p. 25).

Cuttlefish

Iodine block

Spinach leaf

Air-tight container

Seed mixture

Grit

Where to put your budgies' cage

Put the cage high up where budgies feel safe.

Make sure your pets are in a smoke-free place.

Don't use sprays near the cage.

Keep the cage out of bright sunlight.

Drafts will upset your birds.

Make sure other pets can't reach the cage.

Things to get ready

You will need some special equipment to help you care for your new pets. You can find some things around your house, and have fun making others. Make sure you have got all the things ready before you pick up your budgies. Once you have become an experienced bird-keeper, you may want to get an aviary to put in your yard.

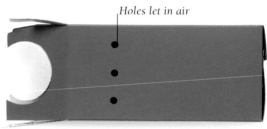
Holes let in air

Carrying box
You will need a small, cardboard carrying box in which to take each of your budgies home.

Cleaning equipment
You will need special things to clean your budgies' cage. Never take things that are used to clean your house. Ask your vet what kind of disinfectant spray to buy.

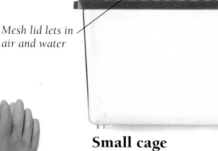
Mesh lid lets in air and water

Small cage
Buy a plastic tank with a mesh lid to put your pets in when you want to clean their cage thoroughly. You can also use the tank when you want to spray your budgies with water (see p. 43).

Bucket

Sponge

Rubber gloves

Detergent

Scrubbing brush

Bottle brush

Scraper

Disinfectant spray

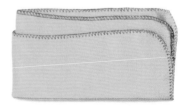

Duster
Get a large, clean duster. You will need to throw this over a bird if it escapes.

Bird toys

Budgies love to play. Find and make toys for them. They will enjoy climbing on an activity center while they are flying free in a room (see p. 36). You can put other small toys in their cage.

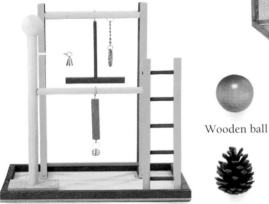

Activity center

Wooden abacus

Wooden ball

Fir cone

The aviary

You can build or buy an outdoor aviary to create a more natural home for your birds. It should have a shed for the birds to shelter in and a large flight area. You can keep many birds together in an aviary (see p. 34).

Plant sprayer

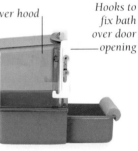

Splash cover hood

Hooks to fix bath over door opening

Birdbath

Bathing equipment

Budgies like to bathe. Buy a bath with a splash cover hood that fits on a door of the cage. Also get a plant sprayer to shower your birds with in the tank.

Weighing scale

You will need to weigh your budgies regularly to check that they are healthy. Find an old, small kitchen scale and paper to line the tray.

Paper tray lining

Fine netting

Rubber suction cups

Free-flying equipment

Get fine netting to put over windows and fireplaces, and rubber suction cups to stick perches onto the walls.

Choosing your birds

A budgie likes company, so you should get at least two to keep in the same cage. You can buy baby budgies, or chicks, from a clutch when they are at least six weeks old. Adult budgies also make good pets, but you must get two that are already good friends. Whichever budgies you choose, check that they are healthy.

Getting two budgies

A budgie will be lonely living on its own. You can choose two males or two females. Males are often easier to tame. Don't worry if you find that you have chosen a male and a female. They are unlikely to have babies in your cage.

Where to get your birds:

🐦 An animal shelter may have birds of all kinds and ages that need new homes.

🐦 A breeder will sell you chicks that are six weeks old.

🐦 A friend's birds may have chicks.

Adult

Chick

Eye has white ring

Plain forehead

Bars run down to beak

Young or old?

It is easy to tell the age of a budgie. It has fine black lines, or bars, down to its beak until it is three months old. An adult budgie has no bars on its forehead and a white ring in its eye.

1 **When you go to choose** your birds, watch the chicks with the owner. Try not to disturb them. Check that the birds are well cared-for. The cage should be clean and hoppers full.

Point to the chicks that you like

Owner tells you about his birds

*Bars on forehead show
the chick is younger
than three months old*

*Chick grips
the owner's
finger tightly*

*Eyes are clear
and shiny*

*Wing feathers are
neat and tidy*

2 **Ask the owner** to catch a
bird that you like, and to tell
you its sex. It should look bright
and alert. Check that the bird is
the right age to be taken home
and that it hasn't been chosen
by someone else.

*Feathers under
the bird's tail
are clean*

3 **Check that the bird** is healthy.
It should have bright eyes, a
smooth beak, and clean feathers all
over its body. Ask the owner to
hold out each of the wings so you
can make sure they aren't damaged.

*Owner carefully lifts
the bird into its box*

*Hold the
carrying
box steady*

*Tightly closed
box contains
your other bird*

4 **The owner will put** the birds
you choose into your special
carrying boxes. Shut the lids
properly so the birds can't escape.
They will breathe the fresh air
that comes in through the
holes. Take your new pets to
your veterinarian on your way
home, so your vet can give
them a check-up.

Welcome home

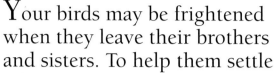 Your birds may be frightened when they leave their brothers and sisters. To help them settle into their new home, have everything prepared in the cage. If you already have a budgie and are introducing a new friend, watch them when they first meet. It is a good idea to cover the cage at first to make your birds feel more relaxed.

Use your scoop to lift the shavings

Lining paper is folded to fit

1 **Fill both of the cage trays** with wood shavings after lining them with paper. The wood shavings and paper will help soak up any spilled water and moist droppings.

Put the perches far apart so that the birds have space to fly

Branch is high, where birds like to perch

2 **Wedge perching** branches between the front and back of the cage. Put one perch high up at each end of the cage and a third perch lower down.

Pour grit until the hopper is full

Hopper is filled with seed mixture

Water seeps into tray until it is full

3 **Pour grit into the grit hopper** after filling the seed hopper and water drinker. Also prepare a selection of fresh food (see p. 25). Put the hoppers and fresh food in the cage. Do not put them under the perches, or bird droppings may fall into them.

Fresh food treats make the birds feel at home

Iodine block is fixed high up in the cage

Millet spray for birds to peck

Bird has settled on a high perch

Birdbath is full of water

Wire cage sits securely on the base

Cuttlefish is clipped to the bars

Water drinker is near a perch

Seed hopper is out of the way of the perch above

Dish of fresh food is on the cage floor

Lined tray slides in and out of the cage base

4 **Release your birds into their cage** when you have finished preparing it. Open each carrying box inside the cage and let your bird climb out. Then spread the cover over the cage. Your birds will feel calmer in dim light and be keener to explore their new home.

Male or female?

Ask your vet to check the sex of your budgies. A young male or cock is larger than a young female or hen. An adult male has a blue cere – a soft, waxy swelling at the top of the beak.

Hen

Cock

Young cock is bigger than young hen

Adult hen has a brown cere

Adult cock has a blue cere

5 **You should arrange** to visit your veterinarian on the way home from picking up your new pets. The vet will examine each bird to make sure that it is healthy.

Vet looks at your bird

Watch carefully as your vet checks your budgie

Feeding your budgies

Like many birds, budgies are omnivores. This means they eat plants as well as meat. In the wild, budgies feed mainly on different kinds of grass seed. They pick up scattered seeds from the ground or peck at flower heads. As well as feeding seed from the hopper, you can scatter some seed on the cage floor.

Seed mixture

Red millet

White millet

Grit

Canary seed

Pour fresh seed into the jam-jar

How much to feed
You should make sure that your birds always have seed to eat. Fill the hopper with seed from the container.

Basic diet
You should feed your pets grit and a specially prepared mixture of seeds that contains essential vitamins and minerals.

When to feed
Check how full the seed hopper is every evening. When the hopper jar is nearly empty, throw away the remaining seed and refill it with enough fresh seed to last your birds about one week.

Your budgie will eat most in the morning and evening

The bird stands on the perch to feed from the hopper

Fresh water
Wild budgerigars get some water from the food they eat, and they also drink from puddles. You must make sure that your pets always have fresh water to drink in their drinker.

Drinker is easily reached from the perch

Budgie can drink whenever it is thirsty

Strong beak is used to crack seeds before they are swallowed

Bird stands on hopper perch

Hopper is filled with grit

Cuttlefish bone contains the mineral calcium, which your birds need to keep healthy

Block contains the essential mineral iodine

Grit

Make sure that the grit hopper is always full. Budgies don't have teeth – they break open the hard seed coats with their beaks. Your budgies swallow grit to help them grind up the tough seeds in their stomachs.

Cuttlefish

Keep a piece of cuttlefish bone clipped to the cage bars. Your budgies will peck the cuttlefish to get any extra calcium that they need. Attach the iodine block to the cage bars for your birds to nibble.

Millet spray

Fresh foods

Fresh fruit and vegetables are full of nutrients. Offer different kinds to your birds to find out which they like best. Clip a spray of dried millet to the cage bars. Your budgie will enjoy pecking seeds from the spray.

Apple   Pear   Raspberries

Alfalfa   Celery   Peas

Tame budgie perches on the tray edge to feed

Carrots   Spinach   Watercress

How much to feed

Once a day, prepare a handful of fruit and vegetables cut into large chunks. Place the chopped-up food on a tray on the cage floor.

Handling your birds

All budgies are frightened of people at first. The more time you spend with your pets, the quicker they will learn to trust you. Start to tame them right away by talking to them. You can train them to perch on your finger. Repeat each of the following steps until your bird is used to it. Then go on to the next.

Budgie is not afraid to peck at food

1 **Wedge a piece** of your budgie's favorite fresh food between the cage bars. Your budgie will not fly away because it will want to nibble the food. It will soon become used to your hand being close to it.

Stroke the feathers gently

Bird pecks at the fresh food

Hold the perch very still

2 **Put your hand** inside the cage while your budgie is eating the food stuck between the bars. Stroke the bird's neck with your finger. It should not be worried by you because it is busy eating. Do not make any sudden hand movements that could startle your bird.

3 **Slowly move a perch** with food clipped on it toward your budgie. Your bird will be tempted onto the perch by the food. It may be shy at first and just put one foot on the perch. Be patient and keep trying.

Holding your birds

Pick up and hold your budgie in cupped hands if you want to look at it closely. It will grip your fingers with its claws. Hold your bird quite firmly to make it feel safe.

Hold firmly but don't squeeze your bird

When to handle your new pets

Days 1-2: Watch your pets carefully but do not disturb them. Keep half of their cage covered.

Day 3: Start to feed your pets by hand through the cage bars. Pick your birds up in cupped hands if you need to.

Days 4-14: Handle your pets several times a day for a short period of time. Follow the handling steps.

After two weeks: Play with your pets and talk to them at least twice a day.

4 **Now your bird** should be ready to sit on your finger instead of the hand-held perch. Move your first finger slowly toward your bird. Your pet should be happy to climb onto your finger.

Claws grip your finger – but it doesn't hurt!

Hold your finger still so your pet finds this new perch stable

Point your finger slightly upward – your pet will move to the highest point of its perch

Budgie waits to be taken out of its cage

5 **When your budgie** is happy to sit on your finger you can take it out of the cage. Make sure the room is safe (see p. 32). If you feel your bird raise its wings, stop moving and let it settle. Now you can begin training your pets to fly to and from your hand.

Understanding your pets

If you watch and listen to your birds carefully, you will soon learn to understand what they are doing. Just like you, budgies keep themselves clean and tidy as well as eat, drink, play, and sleep. In the wild, they splash about in a puddle or stand in the rain when they want to bathe. When one of your budgies wants to wash, it will jump into its bath.

Body feather looks ruffled

Tail feathers are ragged

Molting
At least once a year, your budgies will lose their feathers, or molt. Feathers that are broken or damaged are replaced. Your pets will look very scruffy when they are molting, but they are not ill.

New feathers stick up out of plumage

Wet feathers stick out in all directions

Smooth head is already dry

All puffed up
After having a shower or getting wet in the bath, your budgie moves its body from side to side to shake off the water. It fluffs up its feathers to keep warm. The fluffy feathers make a very warm coat.

Nimble bird can bend to preen under its wing

Preened feathers are sleek

Beak nibbles and strokes feathers back into shape

Preening
You will often see your budgie preening, or cleaning itself with its beak. While preening, your bird spreads a thin layer of oil from a gland under its tail to waterproof its feathers.

28

Gnawing natural perches

Your budgie will peck the bark on its perch looking for insects. Gnawing helps keep its beak from getting too long.

Pointed beak gnaws the bark

Making noises

Budgies make all kinds of sounds. Chicks call to their parents with a loud, high-pitched trill. Happy budgies chirp, but they will stop if disturbed. Budgies are good mimics. They can learn to say words or even imitate a ringing telephone!

Showing friendship

Your two birds will be best friends. They will chirp to each other and play together. You will often see them helping each other groom tricky places.

Budgie bends its head to the side

Budgie nibbles at its friend's neck feathers

Climbing

Like all members of the parrot family, budgies are good climbers. By using its beak as a hook, your budgie can move its feet without falling. Your birds will spend a lot of time climbing the bars of their cage.

Beak grips perch

Claws clasp branch

Budgie tucks its head under a wing

Sleeping

When your budgies are asleep, or roosting, they shut their eyes and fluff up their feathers to keep warm. A sleeping budgie regularly opens its eyes to check it is not in danger.

Cleaning the cage

Your budgies like their home to be very clean. If the cage becomes dirty, it will start to smell and your pets may become ill. You should clean the cage and replace dirty litter, be sure the seed hopper is not blocked, and wash the drinker every day. Throw away uneaten fresh food. Once a week, scrub out the cage thoroughly. Replace any perches that are worn or broken.

Leave the lining paper unless it is torn or very dirty

Use the scraper to remove the dirty litter

1 **Every day**, scrape out any dirty litter from the cage trays. Top up the trays with fresh wood shavings. If you use sand-sheets, replace them daily.

Close your eyes when you blow

Hold the hopper up to your face

2 **Blow the tough seed shells,** called husks, from the seed hopper. Your birds crack the husks off seeds before they eat the seed inside. The husks settle on uneaten seed in the hopper tray.

Push the bottle brush to the end of the tube

Flying husks can make a mess

3 **Clean the inside of the drinker** after throwing away any old water. Then refill the drinker with fresh water.

Close the lid tightly

1 **Once a week**, put your budgies into their small tank. Catch them in cupped hands or by using your duster (see p. 33). Then take out the hoppers, food, and perches. Unclip anything from the bars. Throw away all the wood shavings and lining paper.

Bird can firmly grip the sand-sheet

2 **Scrub the cage trays** with hot, soapy water. Dry them with a paper towel, then spray the insides with the special disinfectant. Leave the trays to dry before refilling them with litter.

Wipe the inside of the jar carefully

Special disinfectant is safe for your birds

Dish-washing liquid

Rubber gloves keep your hands clean

3 **Take out the seed hopper** and throw away any uneaten seed. Wipe the inside of the jar and the hopper tray with a damp sponge before refilling it. Don't forget to clean the fresh food tray.

Scrub all around each of the bars

4 **Clean the cage bars** with soapy water. Then spray them with a little of the disinfectant, and leave them to dry. Put the perches, bath, hoppers, and some fresh food back into the cage. Remember to clip on the cuttlefish and iodine block.

Reach into every corner of the cage

Exercising your budgies

Your birds need regular exercise to keep them healthy. Let them out in a room as soon as they are finger-tame (see p. 26). They should fly freely for at least 20 minutes a day. Make the room safe for your pets by covering all the windows and chimneys with netting. Never let your birds fly outside. If one of your birds won't fly back to its cage, catch it using a duster.

Swing tests bird's sense of balance

Activity center
👥 Ask an adult to help you make an activity center for your birds. Climbing the ladders will strengthen the muscles in their legs and jaws.

Feathers fan out

Eye searches for another perch on which to land

Light body is easily carried by the powerful wings

Wing beats down to lift the bird up and forward

Budgie pushes off the perch with its back feet

Rubber suction cup fixes perch to wall

Ready for take-off
Before you let your birds out of their cage, fix perches high up on the walls of your living room with the suckers. Put newspaper on the floor under the perches. Open the cage door and your birds will fly out. It is fun to watch them flying from perch to perch.

Cover the cage corner that has the highest perch

Throw the duster gently

Glass in windows and doors must be covered with netting.

Screen off fireplaces to stop birds from escaping.

Shut dogs and cats away; they will frighten your birds.

Some houseplants will poison your pets if they eat them.

Heaters and hot drinks may burn your budgies.

Rest after exercise

Cover the cage after your pets have exercised, and when you go to sleep at night. During the day, cover just a corner of the cage. If your pets feel tired, they can sleep in the dark area.

Catching an escaped bird

If your bird doesn't fly back to the cage, turn off the lights. Find your pet and throw the duster over it. Pick it up in the duster and put the bundle in the cage.

Eye judges the distance to the cage

Wing is used as a brake

Body is almost upright

Foot is ready to step onto the cage

Returning home

When your bird is flying freely, leave the cage door open. Put some fresh food inside the cage. This will usually tempt your bird to fly back inside but sometimes it will land on top. Your bird knows exactly how fast to approach its cage. It uses its tail and wings as brakes. By the time it reaches the cage, it has virtually stopped. All it has to do is step onto a perch.

The aviary

Birds love to fly around in an outdoor aviary. There are interesting sounds and things for them to watch. Build an aviary with a weatherproof shelter for your birds to roost in at night. The large flying area, called the flight, should be partly covered with plastic to protect the birds from bad weather. You can keep many birds in an aviary.

Hang the feeder where it isn't in the way of flying birds

Bolt the outer door before opening the inner door into the flight

Birdbath

Tray with grit

Tray with seed mixture

Hanging hopper

Hopper for water

Large mineral block

Aviary equipment

Get a large hanging seed hopper and several trays of different sizes for seed and grit. A shallow bowl will make a good water bath. A hopper can be filled with drinking water.

The aviary

Your aviary should be at least 12 feet (four meters) long and three feet (one meter) wide. You will be able to keep up to 20 budgerigars in this size of aviary. Put fruit-tree branches in the flight and shelter for perches, but make sure you leave your birds plenty of flying room.

Siting the aviary

Make sure other animals can't burrow into the aviary.

Wild birds on overhanging tree may dirty the flight.

Put the aviary in a place sheltered from wind and rain.

A noisy road will upset your birds.

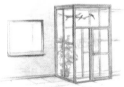

Position the aviary where you can see it from indoors.

Attach the millet spray to the mesh

Plastic protects perch from bad weather

Overhanging, sloping roof keeps shelter dry

Main perch is a branch in a flowerpot

Put the bird-bath under cover

Wire netting stops birds from escaping and other animals from getting in

Shelter should have perches inside for birds to roost on at night

Things to do with your budgies

Look in magazines about birds, or ask your veterinarian for the address of your local pet club. If you join the junior section, you can talk to other bird owners about interesting things to do with your budgies. You can teach a budgie to talk and you can train it to fly back to your finger. Everyone will have good ideas about training your birds and making toys for them.

Bird can fly away if it gets worried

Family pets
Your budgie may make friends with other small pets. A rabbit knows that a bird is too tiny to harm it. Never leave your bird alone with another pet.

Talking budgie
You can try to train your birds to say their names. Whenever you are with one bird on its own, repeat its name over and over again.

Bird hears its name and flies to your finger

Hold your finger high

Bird perches on your hand

Bird cocks its head to one side to listen

Flying to your finger
Every time your birds are flying freely, practice calling them to you. Hold your hand near to where your bird is perching. Repeat its name until it flies onto your finger. In time you should be able to call your bird to you from across the room.

Step closer to the perch if your bird doesn't fly to you

Foot is used to push the ball

Wooden ball

Budgies are very curious. They will be fascinated by anything that moves. Give your birds a small wooden ball and they will play their own sort of carpet soccer!

Budgie stares at the moving disk

Bird slides the disk with its foot

Toy abacus

Make your birds an abacus from a rod and several wooden disks. Your budgies will enjoy shuffling the disks along the rod. Bird toys are special treats – only leave them inside the cage for a short while.

Leaving your pets

Going on vacation

Sometimes you can't take your pets with you when you go on vacation. You must find someone to look after them. You may have a friend who has time to care for your budgies.

What to pack

Get everything ready for your friend. Make sure you pack enough of all the types of food (see p. 24), grit, wood shavings, and lining paper. Don't forget some spare perches and all the cleaning equipment.

Making a checklist

Make a list of all the jobs that need doing every day. Write them down in the order that you do them. Show your friend how to do the complicated jobs. Note the name and telephone number of your vet.

Moving your birds

Take your birds to your friend in their carrying boxes. Take their cage separately. Only allow your friend to let your birds out to exercise if you are sure that they won't be able to escape, and that the windows in the room are covered with netting.

Other kinds of pet birds

You can find out which birds can be kept as pets from your vet. Cockatiels, canaries, and finches are easy to care for. Experienced bird-keepers may train birds of prey. Some people keep racing pigeons; tame chickens and ducks often live in farmyards. Big parrots are pretty birds, but they are happiest living wild.

Feathers on head form a fluffy crest

Thick yellow and white neckband

Gloster fancy canary

Head is raised as canary warbles

Bill is closed when cock sings

Roller canary

Three toes point forward

Yellow cap

Pointed beak is perfect for cracking seeds

Speckled plumage is silky

Lizard canary

Small, round head

Bright yellow plumage

Plump body

Narrow tail

Border fancy canary

Dark eye

Plumage is soft red

Red factor canary

Tail is paler red

Short wing makes canary acrobatic in flight

Canaries
The canary, a type of finch, has been kept as a pet for hundred of years. The cocks sing beautifully. Like all finches, canaries are not as easy to handle as budgies and are difficult to hand-tame. It is best to keep a group of them in an aviary. They enjoy company and are strong fliers.

Cockatiels

Cockatiels belong to a group of small parrots called cockatoos. All cockatoos have a crest on their heads but the cocks and hens look different. Cockatiels are bigger than budgies and need more space. You can keep at least two together in a big cage or aviary. Although more timid than budgies at first, cockatiels are easy to tame.

Bright orange ear patch

Cockatiel hen

Yellow head

Crest can be raised or lowered

Cockatiel cock

Whitish-yellow plumage

Lutino cockatiel cock

Very long tail

Feathery crest

Hooked beak

Pearl markings on long wing

Pearl cockatiel cock

Orange cheek patch

Bright red bill

Gray plumage is duller than the cock's

Black and white stripes on breast

Zebra finch cock

Zebra finch hen

Fawn wings

White breast

Fawn penguin finch cock

Zebra finches

Zebra finches get their name from the black and white stripes on the cock's neck. Like canaries, they are timid birds that should be kept as a group in a very large cage or aviary.

Different kinds of pet birds

Some chickens kept on farms are tamed and kept as pets.

A racing pigeon can find its way home.

A Harris hawk is trained to fly and return.

Lovebirds are often kept by experienced parrot-keepers.

Geese can be aggressive and make good "guard-dogs!"

39

Having babies

Baby birds, called chicks, hatch from eggs laid by their mother. Hen and cock birds won't breed unless you give them a special nesting box. If you have hen and cock budgies, you might think it would be fun to let them have chicks. Don't forget that breeding birds and babies need special care. The chicks will soon grow up and you will need to find them all new homes.

White eggs are the size of a thimble

1 **After mating**, a hen will usually start to lay eggs. She will lay one egg every other day until there are between four and six eggs in the clutch. The hen will sit on the eggs for 18 days to keep them warm.

Egg tooth chips at shell

Hatching chick

Heavy head is propped on an unhatched egg

Two-hour-old chick

Food can be seen in crop

Two-day-old chick

2 **Each chick breaks** through the shell using a tiny chisel-like egg tooth on top of its beak. It rests its head on the unhatched eggs. The hen feeds the chicks food from her mouth and they grow very quickly.

Two-day-old chick is completely smooth

Large bulge of food in crop

Four-day-old chick snuggles up to its older brothers and sisters

Egg has not yet hatched

Six-day-old chick is covered in very fine down

3 **All the hatched** chicks huddle next to one another to keep warm. A new chick is born every two days. The eggs in the clutch hatch out in the same order as they were laid.

Downy feathers start to grow

Weak legs splay out sideways

21 days

23 days

Growing pinfeathers cover head

All the fluffy feathers have now grown

4 **At about 17 days old**, the chicks start to develop their adult feathers. They are now called fledglings. When the youngest chick is 21 days old, the oldest will look like a small, fluffy adult.

25 days

Chick looks almost fully grown

27 days

Black bars run down forehead

Mask has clear spots

Yellow forehead has no bars

6 **After four months**, the budgie molts for the first time. It looks quite spiky as new feathers grow. The bird grooms itself to help the feathers unfold.

5 The chicks are ready to leave the nest and go to new homes at six weeks. They can crack and eat seeds by themselves. They still can't fly properly and are a little bit wobbly when they perch.

Tail is scruffy

Mask spots have grown larger

7 **A budgie is fully adult** after its first molt. A hen can lay eggs of her own when she is five months old. At six months, a white ring develops in each eye, called an iris ring.

Adult feathers are smooth and sleek

Health care

You need to care for your birds properly to make sure that they stay healthy. You must give them the right food (see p. 24), clean out their cage (see p. 30), and make sure they get exercise (see p. 32). You also need to do some health checks with your birds every day. You will learn to spot quickly if a bird is unwell.

Re-clip the cuttlefish if it has slipped

1 Every morning when you take the cover off the cage, check that your birds are alert and active. Make sure that the hoppers and perches are still fixed tightly.

Open the trays to see if the droppings are normal

Budgie looks around curiously

Check that the hopper has not fallen

Head is held between your first and second fingers

2 Look at your budgie's head. The eyes should be bright and shiny and the nostrils clean. Check that the beak is smooth and not overgrown.

Carefully grip the wing between your fingers

3 Gently pull out a wing to check that it is not damaged. Hold the wing in the middle, not at the tip. Examine both sides of the wing. The feathers should be clean and neat.

Tail feathers are in good condition

Claw curls
around your finger

Claw is the
right length

Claw is
too long

*Budgie feels safe
lying in your hand*

*Gently pull
back the tail*

4 Check to see if the claws
are the right length. Hold
your finger under the bird's
foot; the claws will grip it.
Don't forget to check the two
backward-pointing claws.

5 Look under your bird's tail by
tipping it onto its back. The feathers
should be clean and dry. Push back the chest
feathers with your finger to see the pink skin.

*Budgie perches on
the edge of the tray*

*Paper lining
keeps the
tray clean*

*Needle shows
the weight*

Weighing your bird
Weigh your budgie at the
same time on the same day
each week. Write down the
result in your pet diary. If
your budgerigar has lost or
gained a lot of weight, it
may be ill, or it may not be
getting enough exercise.

Weekly shower
When you thoroughly
clean the cage and your
budgies are in their tank,
give them a cool shower.
Use a plant sprayer to
gently spray your birds.
This will keep their
plumage healthy.

Spray produces a fine mist

*Bird stands still to
enjoy its shower*

Your pet care checklist
Use this list to
keep a record
of all the jobs
you need to do.

*Copy this chart. Check
off the jobs when you
have finished them.*

Every day:
Feed your birds
Blow seed husks
from seed hopper
Wash and refill
the drinker
Tidy the cage
and trays
Let birds fly free
Clean underneath
the cage
Examine the eyes,
beak, and nostrils
Look at the wings
Check the claws
◆

Once a week:
Clean the cage
thoroughly
Wash and refill the
seed hopper
Weigh your birds
Shower your pets
Check cuttlefish,
grit, and block
◆

Every year:
Take your budgies
to the veterinarian
for a full check-up

Visiting your veterinarian

The veterinarians who work at your local animal clinic know a lot about pet birds. They will tell you how to care for your birds properly to keep them happy and healthy. You can ask them as many questions as you like. If you think something is wrong with your birds, call your veterinarian immediately. He will try to make them better if they are ill.

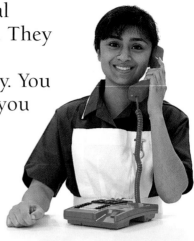

Visiting the vet

Take your budgie to the vet in its carrying box. Bring the cage as well so that the vet can check it. Your vet will give your budgie health checks. If your pet is ill, the vet may give you medicine for your bird or ask you to care for it in a special way.

Telephoning the vet's office

Telephone the veterinary assistant if you want more information about pet clubs or if you think one of your birds is ill. She may suggest you bring your birds to see the vet.

The cage may give the vet a clue about what is wrong with your pet

Budgie is examined all over by the vet

Look carefully at what the vet is doing

Carrying box in which your pet feels safe while traveling

My pet's fact sheet

Try making a fact sheet about each of your birds. Copy the headings on this page or you can make up your own. Then write in the correct information about your bird.

Throat spots

Blue cere

Green chest

Black wing markings

Gray claws

Leave a space to stick in a photograph or draw a picture of each of your pets. Then label all of your pet's special features.

Name: **Charlie**

Birthday: **November 1st**

Weight: **1½ oz. (40g)**

Favorite fresh food: **Spinach**

Best friend: **Tweety**

Veterinarian's name: **Mark Evans**

Vet's office telephone number: **555-1234**

Index